WHEN PLANTS TOOK OVER THE PLANET

Dr Chris Thorogood

Illustrated by
Amy Grimes

Quarto is the authority on a wide range of topics.
Quarto educates, entertains and enriches the lives of
our readers—enthusiasts and lovers of hands-on living.
www.quartoknows.com

© 2021 Quarto Publishing plc
Text © 2021 Chris Thorogood
Illustrations © 2021 Amy Grimes

First published in 2021 by QEB Publishing,
an imprint of The Quarto Group.
26391 Crown Valley Parkway,
Suite 220 Mission Viejo, CA 92691, USA
T: +1 949 380 7510
F: +1 949 380 7575
www.QuartoKnows.com

Editor: Nancy Dickmann
Art Director: Susi Martin
Associate Publisher: Holly Willsher

A CIP record for this book is available from the Library of Congress.

ISBN 978 0 7112 6128 0

Manufactured in Guangdong, China CC052021

9 8 7 6 5 4 3 2 1

MIX
Paper from
responsible sources
FSC
www.fsc.org
FSC® C008047

"My sincere thanks to Sandy
Hetherington for his many helpful
suggestions to improve the book."
C T

"For the team who have worked
together on this book through the
months of lockdown, spent thinking
of the great outdoors."
A G

CONTENTS

WHERE DO PLANTS COME FROM?

Imagine a land without plants. There would be no animals, of course, because animals depend on plants for their existence. But then, about 500 million years ago, something appeared in a pond. It may not have looked like much, but it would change our planet forever! This tiny plant, a type of green alga called a charophyte, was the great-great-great-grandparent of all the incredible plants we see alive today.

The journey begins

Plants moved out of the water onto land about 470 million years ago. It wasn't an easy change, as they needed a protective layer to prevent them from drying out. These land conquerors came in the form of bryophytes—the mosses, liverworts, and hornworts. You can still find them growing in wet places today. Next came lycopods, with advanced plumbing systems that let them tower high above the ground. By 350 million years ago, they formed some of the first forests.

Seeds of success

Stepping out of the prehistoric swamps, look up, and you'll see more familiar trees towering above you. They are the ancestors of the gymnosperms, which include conifers like the ones alive today. Unlike the first land plants, which reproduced using tiny spores, gymnosperms had seeds. Seeds were the key to conquering the land. Seeds could remain dormant until the conditions were right for sprouting, and meant that plants no longer had to stick to wet habitats. There was no stopping plants now!

Plant life blossoms

If a world without plants is too hard to imagine, how about a world without flowers? Over 100 million years ago there was an explosion of color on our green planet. Flowering plants called the angiosperms used color, smell, and sugary rewards to entice insects, animals, and birds to disperse their pollen and seeds, and the landscape started to look very different. Today, flowering plants have turned our planet into a kaleidoscope of color.

CHANGING WITH THE TIMES

Plants were able to conquer the land because of evolution. They evolved gradually, through tiny changes, over many generations. But just as in all living things, a plant does not choose to evolve. Instead, random changes to its genes may control how the plant grows—these are called mutations. Most mutations make the plant less likely to survive. But just once in a while, a mutation gives the plant an advantage—for example, enabling it to grow in a new type of habitat. The plant will pass on the new mutation to its offspring. We call this process natural selection.

Plants today

Look out for the magnifying glass to see where in the world you can find the plants.

Fossil forests

Are you ready to go on a prehistoric plant safari? We're going to swim through ancient swamps, climb towering trees, and trek through the very first fossil forests, in search of the ancestors of today's plants. Along the way, we'll examine living examples too, piecing together the jigsaw of plant evolution. As you uncover each group of plants, see if you can spot the changes that led to their success.

OUR GREEN PLANET

Our planet wasn't always green. In fact, it once looked very different! It has changed dramatically over a long period of time. Life only began when Earth became cool and stable enough to support it—about three and a half billion years ago.

A timeline of plants on Earth

It's difficult to get your head around the past when you're talking about billions of years! To make it easier, scientists divide the Earth's history into chunks. The largest chunk is called an eon. Eons are subdivided into eras, eras into periods, periods into epochs, and epochs into ages. Each section is defined by the types of rocks, plants, and animals that existed at the time.

Set in stone?

Over hundreds of millions of years, plant life became more complex, because of the process of evolution. This simplified diagram shows some of the important groups of plants that evolved over time, starting with the oldest at the bottom, and the youngest at the top. This reflects the way in which their fossils are found laid down in rocks, with the youngest rocks at the top of the stack.

Remember that for most of these groups, there are still descendants living today. For example, mosses may have evolved long before the first flowers, but there are still many mosses alive today. This means that they are descendants of a very ancient group.

millions of years ago	Era	Period
2.6	Cenozoic	Quaternary
23	Cenozoic	Neogene
66	Cenozoic	Paleogene
145	Mesozoic	Cretaceous
210	Mesozoic	Jurassic
252	Mesozoic	Triassic
299	Paleozoic	Permian
359	Paleozoic	Carboniferous
419	Paleozoic	Devonian
444	Paleozoic	Silurian
485	Paleozoic	Ordovician

Flowering plants
becoming dominant

Flowering plants appearing
about 130 MYA

Cycads appearing
about 280 MYA

Gymnosperms
appearing about
320 MYA

Lycopods and horsetails
appearing about
350 MYA

Ferns appearing
about 400 MYA

Bryophytes appearing about 470 MYA

Algae appearing
about 500 MYA

Leefructus

WHERE DID PLANT FOSSILS COME FROM?

Plant fossils are the remains of plants that died long ago, but were preserved in rock. These fossils can be many millions of years old. Some preserved very well, giving scientists clues about how the plants looked and behaved. Others were very delicate, and preserved poorly, or only as fragments. By examining both fossils of plants that existed long ago, alongside plants that are alive today, we can piece together the complicated jigsaw of plant evolution. Each time we discover a new species, it provides a more complete understanding of how plants evolved, and what preceded the ones alive today—like adding pieces to a jigsaw puzzle.

Horsetail

THE PLANT FAMILY TREE

The timeline on the previous page shows us when each of the various groups of plants first appeared, but it doesn't show how the different groups of plants are related to each other. It's time to put them on a giant family tree!

The plant tree of life

Charles Darwin (1809-82) was one of the first scientists to explain how evolution works. In his book *On The Origin of Species*, published in 1859, he explained how evolution requires both mutation and natural selection. Darwin's ideas meant that rather than thinking about living things evolving in a single line, we can imagine it taking the form of a tree, with new lines of species branching off in different directions. The diagram on this page is a very simple "tree of life" that focuses on the plants discussed in this book.

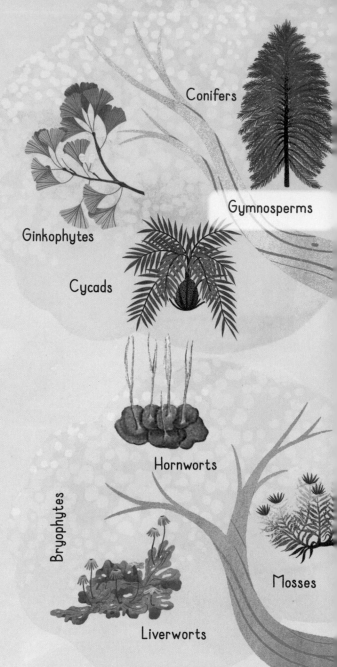

Conifers

Gymnosperms

Ginkophytes

Cycads

Hornworts

Bryophytes

Mosses

Liverworts

BREAKING THE CODE

To explain how species are related, they are put into groups called orders, families, and genera. For centuries, people relied on a living thing's appearance to decide what group to put it into. But this method could be unreliable, because plants that may look very similar are not necessarily related. Today, plants are classified using DNA—their genetic code. By examining the differences in the sequences of DNA, scientists have been able to identify the evolutionary relationships among all the major groups of plants. Each group of related plants, known as a clade, evolved over time from a single ancestral plant—known as the common ancestor.

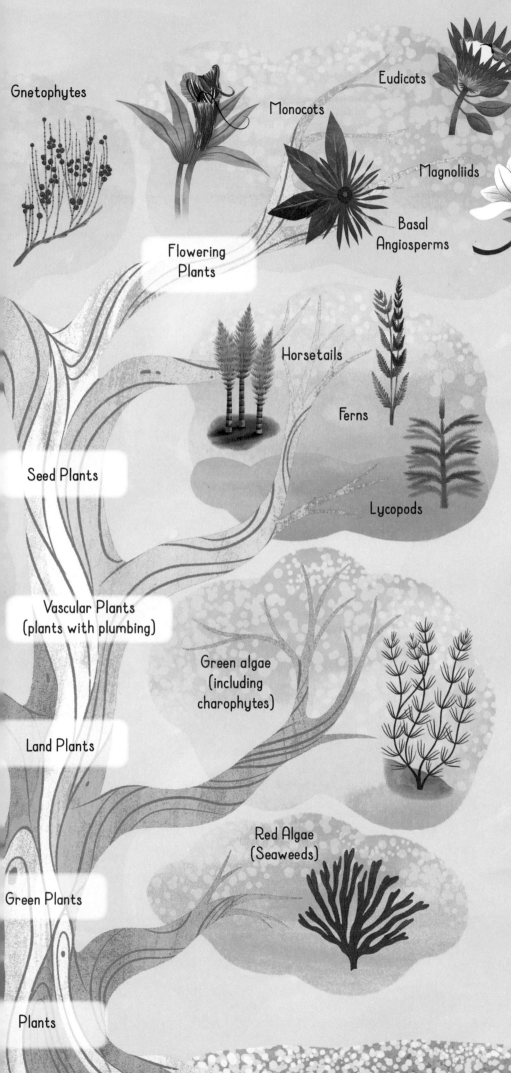

Gnetophytes

Eudicots

Monocots

Magnoliids

Flowering
Plants

Basal
Angiosperms

Horsetails

Ferns

Lycopods

Seed Plants

Vascular Plants
(plants with plumbing)

Green algae
(including
charophytes)

Land Plants

Red Algae
(Seaweeds)

Green Plants

Plants

Scientific names

All species have a unique scientific name made up of two words, which is written in italics. The first word describes the genus— the group to which all the most closely related species belong. The second word describes the particular species. In this book, only the genus name is given, unless several species from the same genus are described side by side. Sometimes whole groups called orders are described together. These end in "-ales" and do not appear in italics. These names can seem complicated, but each has a guide to help you pronounce them properly.

What does "MYA" mean?

You'll notice the letters "MYA" after many of the dates in this book. MYA is short for "millions of years ago." These dates are worked out by dating fossils. In many cases, there isn't a lot to go on, and the dates are approximate. Living species appear throughout the book to show you how the plants you see today are related to those that are known only from fossils.

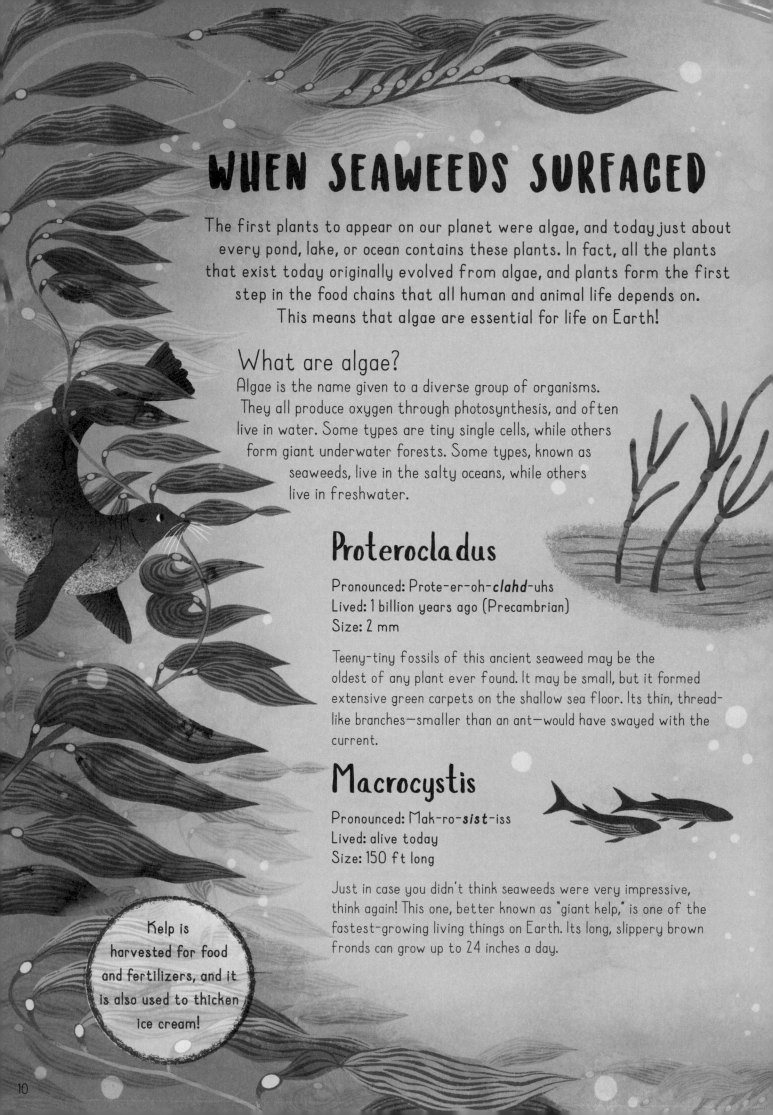

WHEN SEAWEEDS SURFACED

The first plants to appear on our planet were algae, and today just about every pond, lake, or ocean contains these plants. In fact, all the plants that exist today originally evolved from algae, and plants form the first step in the food chains that all human and animal life depends on. This means that algae are essential for life on Earth!

What are algae?

Algae is the name given to a diverse group of organisms. They all produce oxygen through photosynthesis, and often live in water. Some types are tiny single cells, while others form giant underwater forests. Some types, known as seaweeds, live in the salty oceans, while others live in freshwater.

Proterocladus

Pronounced: Prote-er-oh-*clahd*-uhs
Lived: 1 billion years ago (Precambrian)
Size: 2 mm

Teeny-tiny fossils of this ancient seaweed may be the oldest of any plant ever found. It may be small, but it formed extensive green carpets on the shallow sea floor. Its thin, thread-like branches—smaller than an ant—would have swayed with the current.

Macrocystis

Pronounced: Mak-ro-*sist*-iss
Lived: alive today
Size: 150 ft long

Just in case you didn't think seaweeds were very impressive, think again! This one, better known as "giant kelp," is one of the fastest-growing living things on Earth. Its long, slippery brown fronds can grow up to 24 inches a day.

Kelp is harvested for food and fertilizers, and it is also used to thicken ice cream!

Sargassum

Pronounced: Sarg-**ass**-uhm
Lived: alive today
Size: several yards long

Sargassum is named after a part of the Atlantic Ocean called the Sargasso Sea, where this seaweed forms vast, brown patches in the calm blue water. They form an important habitat for fish and turtles, which shelter among the seaweed fronds.

Some *Sargassum* islands are so large that they can be seen from space!

FLOATING FORESTS

Some types of seaweed, including giant kelp, have root-like parts that anchor them to the sea floor. They allow the kelp to form vast kelp forests, with gas-filled bladders that keep the fronds afloat. Other types of seaweed, including some forms of *Sargassum*, never touch the sea floor. They just drift with the current.

Padina

Pronounced: Pah-**deen**-a
Lived: alive today
Size: up to 4 in

This beauty is commonly known as the "peacock's tail." Coiled, fan-shaped fronds with curly edges spiral out from its center. It is widespread in shallow water across the Pacific, Atlantic, and Indian Oceans, as well as in the Mediterranean.

Look for Padina in rock pools at low tide.

Palmophyllales

Pronounced: Pal-mof-ill-**ahl**-eez
Lived: alive today
Size: up to 20 in across

Plants need sunlight to make their own food, so most seaweeds live on the surface or in shallow waters. But these mysterious seaweeds grow in the dark depths, as far as 660 feet down. One form has umbrella-like fronds that are perfect for capturing the dim light.

ASTONISHING ALGAE

Now let's head inland to investigate the many different forms of freshwater green algae. Often called "pondweed," they grow in lakes, rivers, and ponds. The charophytes are an important group that has been around for about 450-500 million years, and some types have changed very little. It may seem astonishing, but large land plants all evolved from the ancestors of these seemingly simple green algae.

This tiny fossil charophyte was uncovered in a formation called the "Rhynie chert" in Aberdeenshire, in Scotland. Chert is a kind of rock that formed mostly of a glassy mineral called quartz. In the Rhynie chert, whole communities of ancient plants and animals were preserved in remarkable detail. This one is probably the great-great-great-grandparent to many of the charophytes we see living today.

Paleonitella

Pronounced: Pale-ee-yo-ni-*tell*-a
Lived: 400 MYA (Devonian)
Size: unknown

Rinistachya

Pronounced: Rin-is-*stah*-kee-ya
Lived: 370 MYA (Devonian)
Size: 3 in

Fossils of this algae were discovered in the black shales of the Witpoort Formation in South Africa. With its loose, feathery whorls, this species wouldn't have looked too dissimilar to the freshwater algae you might see today, an incredible 370 million years later!

Chara

Pronounced: *Kah*-ra
Lived: alive today
Size: up to several yards

This plant anchors itself to the muddy beds of rivers and lakes, and its feathery fronds form great green clouds under the water's surface. Like other charophytes, it plays an important role in keeping the habitat it lives in healthy, providing a green oasis for pond life, and keeping the water clean and clear.

Drying out

Charophytes have been around for hundreds of millions of years—long before humans arrived. Left to their own devices, they thrive. However, many species are under severe threat of extinction due to the loss of their watery habitats. Some of this is a result of human activity.

LIFE THROUGH A LENS

Some freshwater algae are so tiny that we cannot even see them with the naked eye. But under the microscope, a whole new world comes into focus—a world of beautiful, delicate organisms that we may walk past every day without even knowing.

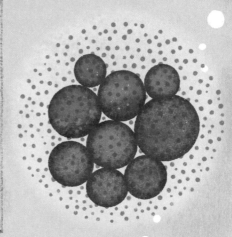

Synurales

Pronounced: Sine-your-*rah*-leez
Lived: 157 MYA–present (Jurassic to today)
Size: microscopic

These tiny algae were identified nearly two centuries ago by a German scientist who used a microscope to see their complicated beauty. Some types are covered in tiny scales and spines, while others live in blackberry-shaped colonies. By examining the different species in mud from the bottom of lakes, scientists have been able to see how conditions have changed over time.

Volvox

Pronounced: Vol-vox
Lived: alive today
Size: microscopic

There are even microscopic algae lurking in the puddles at our feet, and some are particularly beautiful. This tiny "puddle plant" forms studded spheres in stagnant ponds, puddles, and ditches. It has special structures, called flagella, which are like tiny tails that help it to swim towards the light.

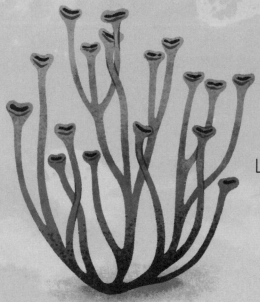

WHEN PLANTS CONQUERED LAND

Look at a stone wall, a path, or a tree and you will discover a whole world teeming with life—a miniature forest of plants called bryophytes. These include mosses, but you may also see liverworts with flat, creeping fronds and hornworts, which have strange horn-like structures. About 470 years ago, these small plants and their relatives left the water and conquered land.

Cooksonia

Pronounced: Cook-*sone*-ee-a
Lived: 433–393 MYA (Silurian to Devonian)
Size: about an inch tall

This fossil plant was small and simple. It didn't have leaves, flowers, or roots, but it did have a special transport tissue called xylem. The xylem enabled it to take up water from the soil, transporting it to other parts of the plant. This means that Cooksonia was actually more closely related to the taller vascular plants we see living today. It holds clues to how plants conquered land.

Sphagnum

Pronounced: *Sphag*-noom
Lived: alive today
Size: blankets to about 12 in deep

This moss has a trick up its sleeve: it has an incredible water-storing capacity—squeeze a clump of it and you will see just how much it can hold! It forms soft green blankets in bogs and other cool, wet places. As the moss decays, it forms peat.

Sphagnum is too acidic for bacteria to grow in it, so it was once used as a dressing for wounds.

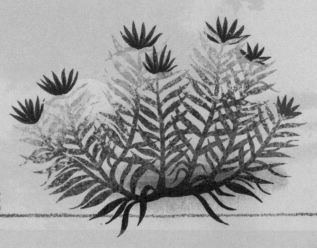

POWERFUL PEAT

Too much CO_2 in the atmosphere contributes to climate change, but peat stores huge amounts of CO_2. This means that peat bogs may be crucial for combating climate change. Sadly, peat bogs around the world are being destroyed—either to drain the land for farming, or to use the peat as fuel.

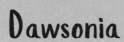

Dawsonia

Pronounced: Door-*sone*-ee-a
Lived: alive today
Size: up to 24 in high

This extraordinary moss is the tallest in the world, towering above the other mosses. This "muscular moss" has special tubes or vessels that let it move water over greater distances. With these tubes, this moss has managed to do what no other moss can: stand tall.

Zosterophyllum

Pronounced: Zost-er-oh-*fill*-uhm
Lived: 400 MYA (Devonian)
Size: up to about 12 in tall

Zosterophyllum was a peculiar looking plant covered in little spines and coiled branches. Like *Cooksonia*, it was one of the first to have a "plumbing system" of veins, like most of the plants and trees we see around us today. It was another stepping-stone to a group of more complicated plants: the lycopods.

Spore factories

Bryophytes reproduce using spores, not seeds. Their spore-containing structures can come in all shapes and sizes! Those of *Marchantia* look like crowds of tiny green umbrellas.

Marchantia

Pronounced: Mark-*ant*-ee-a
Lived: alive today
Size: ground-level

This little land conqueror is a form of liverwort of which there are thousands of different species. They are common in damp, shady places, where they form emerald-colored carpets with creeping, finger-like fronds. People once thought that the plant's liver-like shape meant that it could cure liver diseases. Liverworts are important for holding soil together, such as on riverbanks.

LOST LYCOPODS

Lycopods are the most ancient group of vascular plants still alive. They were among the first to grow roots, stems, and leaves like the plants we see on land today. Those species still living today are small, but 350 million years ago, their ancestors were towering trees with long finger-like leaves. Just imagine peering up into the canopy of a forest of lycopods like these!

Lepidodendron

Pronounced: Lep-id-oh-**den**-dron
Lived: 388-209 MYA (Devonian to Triassic)
Size: 100 ft high

Lepidodendron was truly a goliath. Its giant broccoli-like canopy emerged from an enormous trunk that could grow over 100 feet high, with a width of 6.5 feet at its base. Its needle-like leaves sprouted directly from the trunk in great green spirals. When they fell, they left diamond-shaped scars along the trunk. Like other lycopods, *Lepidodendron* had spores. They were produced in cone-like structures at the tips of the branches.

Baragwanathia

Pronounced: Bar-rag-wan-**aa**-thee-ya
Lived: 427-393 MYA (Silurian to Devonian)
Size: 3 ft high

Baragwanathia was among the very first plants to grow true leaves and strong tubes for taking up nutrients and water from the soil. It was advanced for its time, and larger than the other plants on land—about the size of a small bush. Its descendants were to shoot upwards and cover the Earth in great green forests.

Sigillaria

Pronounced: Sih-jill-**ah**-rhee-a
Lived: 388–254 MYA (Devonian to Permian)
Size: 100 ft high

Sigillaria fossils have been found all around the world. They show that the plant had a fat, scaly trunk topped with spiky foliage. The trunk looked tree-like, but it was made up of closely packed leaf bases, not wood. *Sigillaria* may have had a short life cycle—growing rapidly, and reaching maturity in just a few years. Like sphagnum moss, its remains formed peat, and this peat eventually turned into coal.

Protolepidodendropsis

Pronounced: Proh-toh-lepido-den-**drop**-sis
Lived: 380 MYA (Late Devonian)
Size: 6.5–13 ft high

To this day we are still discovering extinct plants. *Protolepidodendropsis* was found in the sandstone of Svalbard—a group of Arctic islands that was once located on the equator. The plants sprouted in strange-looking thickets spaced apart from one another, forming miniature forests about 13 feet high. Their trunks were only 4 inches wide and were swollen at the base. *Protolepidodendropsis* is a reminder that there are still fossil plants waiting to be unearthed. What strange discoveries may still be ahead?

Selaginella lepidophylla grows in hot, dry parts of Mexico and North America.

Selaginella lepidophylla

Pronounced:
Sell-a-jin-**ell**-ah leh-pid-oh-**phill**-ah
Lived: alive today
Size: ground level

This incredible desert survivor can live for years without any rainwater at all! Known as the resurrection plant, it curls up in dry weather—sometimes for years. When the rain returns, it springs back to life, unfurling and turning green within just a few hours.

WHEN LEAVES UNFOLDED

The earliest leaves in the fossil record are special structures called microphylls, like those of some lycopods. About 350 million years ago, plants evolved a new type of leaf called a megaphyll. Megaphyll leaves are more complex, typically with many veins, and may have evolved from branches. The evolution of leaves would change the atmosphere and life on Earth forever.

Rhynia

Pronounced: *Rine*-ee-ah
Lived: 411–408 MYA (Devonian)
Size: about an inch

But first, let's look at a fossil plant that *didn't* have leaves. Even so, this little plant was advanced for its time, with some features more like the ferns and seed plants. Perhaps the leaves of these plants evolved from the branches of something like those of *Rhynia*. *Rhynia* was found in the Rhynie chert in Aberdeenshire, Scotland, where it grew near hot springs.

TURNING OVER A NEW LEAF

It's fascinating to think that the extraordinary diversity of leaves we see all around us today may have started out with the simple megaphylls of plants like *Eophyllophyton*. Fossils give clues to how leaves first appeared. In *Tetraxylopteris* and *Psilophyton*, fossils show branches becoming flattened and webbing connecting the gaps between them. This may have eventually led to the formation of larger, flatter leaves.

Eophyllophyton

Pronounced: Ee-oh-file-oh-*phyte*-on
Lived: 383–410 MYA (Devonian)
Size: leaves up to ¼ in long

This is the oldest known plant to have "turned over a new leaf," producing megaphylls. At just ¼ inch long, its leaves were tiny. They grew in pairs, with branched veins running through them. Some appear to have been webbed, and they fanned out at different angles. The spores grew in little clusters on the under surface of the leaves, rather like they do in ferns.

Tetraxylopteris

Pronounced: Tetra-zy-*lop*-ter-is
Lived: 390–360 MYA (Devonian)
Size: possibly to about 20 in

This curious fossil plant grew as an intricate mass, made up of a main stem and branches forking out in opposite directions. The evolution of megaphyll leaves would have a major impact on the global environment, and perhaps plants like this hold clues as to how this process began.

Psilophyton

Pronounced: Sile-oh-*fite*-on
Lived: 410–315 MYA (Devonian)
Size: to about 24 in

Fossils of this plant have been found in North America, Europe, and China. It lived at about the same time as *Rhynia* but it has a more complicated structure. There are lots of branches ending in blunt tips, and a strong "plumbing system" to pump water. At the top of the plant, the branches produced clusters of spores that were released through slits.

Psilotum

Pronounced: Sile-*oh*-toom
Lived: alive today
Size: up to about 12 in

Now for another plant without leaves—only this time, it is a plant that has lost them! Often called "whisk ferns," these strange plants were once thought to be living survivors of ancient groups of plants that had not yet evolved leaves, like *Rhynia*, *Tetraxylopteris* and *Psilophyton*. But by examining the plants' DNA, scientists have shown that, in fact, *Psilotum* is more closely related to the horsetails and ferns.

WHEN FERNS UNFURLED

It's time to explore the beginnings of an important plant group: the ferns. These familiar and often very beautiful plants first unfurled in the Devonian period, about 400 million years ago.

All change

The appearance of ferns marked a period of major change on our planet. Ferns became one of the most important groups of plants on Earth in the Carboniferous period, about 300 million years ago. Alongside the giant tree-like lycopods, these plants formed vast green swamps around the world.

Wattieza

Pronounced: Wot-ee-*ehz*-a
Lived: 388–84 MYA (Devonian)
Size: up to 26 ft

Wattieza are among the earliest known trees, belonging to a group of plants that were likely to have been the ancestors of the ferns and horsetails. They grew to 26 feet tall, resembling the tree ferns that are alive today. The trees may have produced lots of leaf litter, providing a carpet of detritus that allowed animals to flourish.

Phlebopteris

Pronounced: Fleb-*op*-ter-is
Lived: 250–66 MYA (Triassic to Cretaceous)
Size: leaves about 8 in long

This unusual-looking fern once formed vast swathes of leafy umbrellas over the green landscape. Its leaves grew from underground stems that spread outward across the forest floor in a network. *Phlebopteris* lived on every continent, including Antarctica. Living relatives of this fossil fern survive in parts of Southeast Asia.

FROZEN IN TIME

Some ferns, such as *Phlebopteris* and *Todites*, are very well preserved in the fossil record. Others, such as the *Wattieza* stumps that were found rooted in position in New York, show us how they grew when they were alive. The later discovery of fossils of the upper parts of the tree gave an even more complete picture. Meanwhile, the oval-shaped markings on fossils of *Psaronius* show how the leaves were attached to the plant.

Compsognathus

Todites

Pronounced: Tod-*ite*-eez
Lived: 250–61 MYA (Triassic to Paleogene)
Size: leaf divisions (pinnae) 12 in long

This isn't any old fossil fern—it belongs to
a group called the royal fern family, which
includes over 20 species that are still alive
today. Its closest living relatives, a group called
Todea, includes a species that still grows in
South Africa, New Zealand, and Australia,
and another that grows in Papua New Guinea.
Todites looked rather like a small tree fern,
with large, floppy green fronds spraying out
from the top of its slender trunk.

Claytosmunda

Pronounced: Clay-toz-*mun*-dah
Lived: 180 MYA–present (Jurassic to today)
Size: 3 ft

This fern, which still exists today, is
sometimes called the "interrupted fern"
because of its unusual gappy leaves.
Amazingly, this fern's overall form just
hasn't changed—fossils from 180 million
years ago look just like the plants you can
find today. So you really can walk through a
living fossil forest without a time machine!

Psaronius

Pronounced: Sah-*roh*-nee-uhs
Lived: 360–300 MYA (Devonian to
Carboniferous)
Size: 26–33 ft tall

Here is a handsome fossil fern that, like
Wattieza, reached tree-like proportions,
towering to 33 feet tall. It had a vast, fat
trunk up to 3 feet wide. Its beautiful green
fronds sprayed out from the top, expanding
from soft, coiled buds called croziers.

The leaves of
Psaronius grew to
10 feet long.

FLOURISHING FERNS

Ferns first unfurled in the Devonian period, but it wasn't until the start of the Cretaceous that many of today's fern families began to flourish. Now ferns are one of the largest and most diverse groups of plants around. There are some 10,000 species of them growing around the world.

Here, there, and everywhere

Ferns are not all alike. Some have large fronds, or grow into towering trees, while others are the size of a fingernail. Tropical ferns can grow very quickly, while tree ferns in cooler places often grow much more slowly. This diversity has led to their success, allowing ferns to flourish in many different habitats.

Fossil fronds tell us that ferns similar to *Cyathea* were alive over 100 million years ago.

Azolla

Pronounced: *Az*-oll-a
Lived: alive today
Size: 1/5 in

Now for the cutest fern! This tiny fern looks far more like pondweed or a moss, and it spends its entire life floating on the water's surface, where it can form vast green carpets. It grows extremely fast, which can be a problem, as it chokes other pond life. Not so cute after all!

Cyathea

Pronounced: Sie-*ath*-ee-a
Lived: 237 MYA-present (Silurian to today)
Size: 50 ft

These tree ferns grow in cool wet woods as well as tropical rainforests. Their long, slender trunks tower above the other plants, with great nodding green fronds radiating out from the top. The leaves alone can be several yards long! One of this fern's relatives has an amazing name: the flying spider-monkey tree fern!

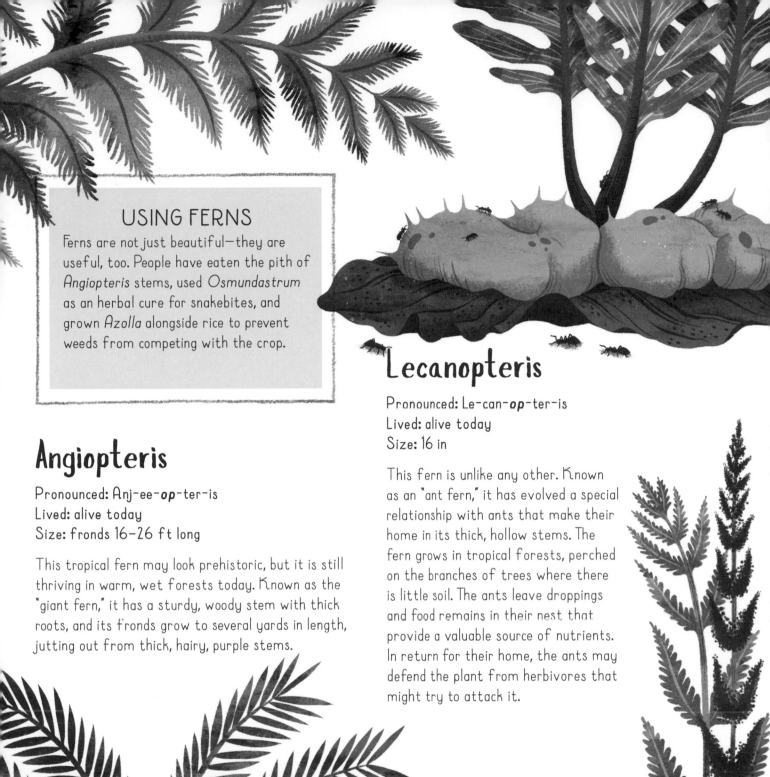

Lecanopteris

Pronounced: Le-can-**op**-ter-is
Lived: alive today
Size: 16 in

This fern is unlike any other. Known as an "ant fern," it has evolved a special relationship with ants that make their home in its thick, hollow stems. The fern grows in tropical forests, perched on the branches of trees where there is little soil. The ants leave droppings and food remains in their nest that provide a valuable source of nutrients. In return for their home, the ants may defend the plant from herbivores that might try to attack it.

Angiopteris

Pronounced: Anj-ee-**op**-ter-is
Lived: alive today
Size: fronds 16–26 ft long

This tropical fern may look prehistoric, but it is still thriving in warm, wet forests today. Known as the "giant fern," it has a sturdy, woody stem with thick roots, and its fronds grow to several yards in length, jutting out from thick, hairy, purple stems.

Osmundastrum

Pronounced: Oz-mund-**ast**-room
Lived: alive today
Size: 5 ft

Osmundastrum grows in swamps and moist woodlands in the Americas and east Asia. Sometimes it forms vast colonies on the forest floor where it spreads by means of wiry, hairy roots. It sends up cinnamon-colored spore-bearing fronds that poke out from the leafy rosettes like long, brown tongues.

WHEN HORSETAILS WERE HUGE

For over 100 million years, these curious plants ruled the world. Also called "snake grasses," and "puzzle grasses," the twenty or so species of horsetails that remain alive today are living fossils—remnants of once-towering forests.

Prehistoric forests

Some horsetails grew to a colossal 100 feet tall. Can you imagine wandering among fat pole-like trunks of giant horsetails like the ones on these pages, with their bristly fronds stretching out high above your head? They are gone, but not forgotten—their remains were buried and eventually turned into coal deposits.

Sphenophyllum

Pronounced: Sfeen-oh-*phill*-uhm
Lived: 383–252 MYA (Devonian to Triassic)
Size: 3 ft

If *Sphenophyllum* was alive today, you might have to fight your way through a thicket of these! Rather than growing into huge trees like some of its cousins that formed the canopy of the fossil forests, this plant was part of the understorey. Its brittle, jointed stems may have been vine-like, creeping through the undergrowth.

Pseudobornia

Pronounced: ss-yood-oh-*born*-ee-ya
Lived: 383–359 MYA (Devonian)
Size: 50–66 ft

This early horsetail was discovered in the late 1800s, but it wasn't until a century later that scientists realized that the fossils belonged to a large tree up to about 66 feet high. The tree had a thick, straight central trunk and many leafy branches sticking out. This tree was thriving when the first salamander-like animals with four limbs appeared, and when armored prehistoric fish swam the oceans.

Neocalamites

Pronounced: Nee-oh-ca-la-*mite*-eez
Lived: ca. 299–151 MYA (Carboniferous to Jurassic)
Size: up to 6.5 ft

Like many other horsetails, this plant thrived in wet and humid places, such as near lakes and rivers. *Neocalamites* had rush-like stems with parallel ribs running up them. Fossils of this plant have been found in China and Australia, as well as in parts of Europe. One form had downward-pointing prickles that probably protected the plant from hungry herbivores.

Arthropitys

Pronounced: Arth-rop-*pit*-iss
Lived: 318–247 MYA (Carboniferous to Triassic)
Size: up to 50 ft

Many plant fossils are just fragments—bits and pieces of hollow stem, or the occasional leafy shoot here and there. But an especially large fossil horsetail was once found in Germany, helping scientists to fill in the gaps. Unlike other giant horsetails, *Arthropitys* had many branches. This feature might have allowed it to compete with the gymnosperms that would soon appear.

WHAT'S IN A NAME?

A plant's scientific name often gives a clue about its appearance. For example, *Sphenophyllum* comes from the Greek words for "wedge" and "leaf." They describe the typical shape of the leaf, which resembles a fan.

Calamites

Pronounced: Cal-ah-*mite*-eez
Lived: 359–315 MYA (Devonian to Carboniferous)
Size: up to about 65 ft

These giant horsetails once covered vast areas of swamps and sandy riverbanks. From a distance, they may have looked like a stand of pine trees, but on closer inspection you would see that their large, pole-like stems looked more like bamboo. These trees had massive underground runners that allowed them to spread, and to sprout new stems if they were damaged.

Pederpes

LIVING FOSSILS

Horsetails were once widespread, providing food for hungry dinosaurs. Many species are still alive today, and they are remarkably similar to their long-lost ancestors, if a lot smaller. These modern horsetails have remained largely unchanged, so we call them "living fossils."

What changed?
Horsetails formed fast-growing, bamboo-like thickets that blanketed the Earth's swamps for hundreds of millions of years. Eventually these forests thinned out, and horsetails were replaced by flowering plants. A changing climate and drier land may have led many species to extinction.

These living fossils can be found all around the world.

Equisetum myriochaetum

Pronounced: Eck-whiz-*eet*-uhm mir-ee-oh-*keet*-uhm
Lived: alive today
Size: 16.5 ft

This giant living fossil is one of the tallest modern horsetail species. It is native to the Americas, and it is sometimes planted in botanical gardens as an example of a living "fossil forest." The plant sends up many tall, narrow shoots, with widely spaced brown bands from which whorls of spidery green leaves poke out. It can grow in large stands, which are rather beautiful.

Equisetum giganteum

Pronounced: Eck-whiz-*eet*-uhm ji-*gant*-ee-uhm
Lived: alive today
Size: 6.5–16.5 ft

To stand in a forest of "giant horsetail" is about the closest we can get to experiencing what the prehistoric forests were like. This species can reach an impressive height of 16.5 feet, but when supported by other plants, some stems can grow much longer. The rush-like stems are small and slender—only an inch or so across.

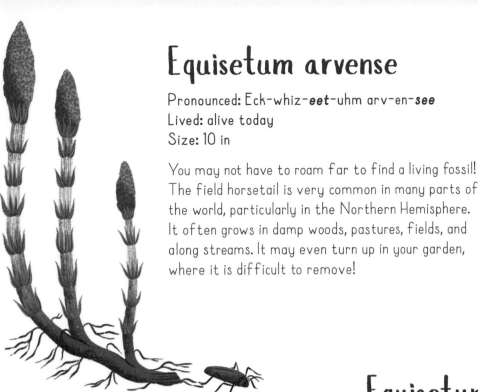

Equisetum arvense

Pronounced: Eck-whiz-*eet*-uhm arv-en-*see*
Lived: alive today
Size: 10 in

You may not have to roam far to find a living fossil!
The field horsetail is very common in many parts of
the world, particularly in the Northern Hemisphere.
It often grows in damp woods, pastures, fields, and
along streams. It may even turn up in your garden,
where it is difficult to remove!

Equisetum telmateia

Pronounced: Eck-whiz-*eet*-uhm tel-*matt*-eeh-yah
Lived: alive today
Size: 5 ft

This horsetail is similar to the field horsetail, but about
four times larger. Like its smaller cousin, it produces
yellow-brown spore-bearing stems early in the spring.
Later in the year, the plant produces green feathery
foliage. The stems are banded with blackish rings at the
base, and are lush and leafy toward the tips.

HANDY HORSETAILS

Horsetails have been used for various purposes
around the world and throughout history—for
example, as thickening powders, to fatten
geese, for fibers, and for herbal medicines. The
shoots of the plant *Equisetum arvense* were
eaten like asparagus by the Romans.

Equisetum hyemale

Pronounced: Eck-whiz-*eet*-uhm hi-*mahl*-eh
Lived: alive today
Size: 3 ft

This horsetail has black-banded stems and grows
in soggy places such as lake and pond margins,
ditches, and swamps. It is widespread across
the Northern Hemisphere. *Equisetum hymale* is
sometimes called the "scouring rush" because its
stems contain a hard substance called silica that
makes them good for scouring and polishing.

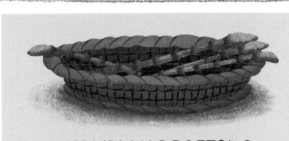

WHEN SEED PLANTS SURFACED

It's time to step out of the horsetail thickets, lycopod swamps, and fern prairies to enter a very different kind of forest. Those plants produced tiny spores, and needed water to reproduce. But now we'll take a closer look at some of the very first plants to evolve seeds. They would transform our planet forever!

Seeds of change

Seeds are like baby plants stored in a protective outer coating. They can remain dormant for long periods. Plants that produced seeds didn't necessarily have to live in permanently wet habitats. They could colonize other parts of the planet.

Archaeopteris

Pronounced: Ark-ee-*op*-terris
Lived: 384–299 MYA (Devonian to Carboniferous)
Size: 33 ft

Until the discovery of *Wattieza*, fern-like *Archaeopteris* was thought to be the first plant to resemble the trees that are alive today. It had long roots, produced buds, and had a woody, branched trunk. However, *Archaeopteris* produced spores rather than seeds. It is thought to be an early step in the evolution of a group called the seed ferns.

SEED FERNS

The first plants to produce seeds instead of spores looked a little like ferns, so they are often called "seed ferns." The seed ferns were among the first plants to colonize drier habitats, and they are the ancestors of the plants that dominate nearly every habitat on Earth today.

Elkinsia

Pronounced: Ell-*kin*-see-ah
Lived: 370–360 MYA (Devonian)
Size: less than 3 ft

This plant was one of the earliest seed ferns. *Elkinsia* grew to about the size of a fennel plant, with large, floppy leaves that spiraled up the stems. Seeds and pollen were arranged in clusters at the top. Plants like this were common by the Late Devonian—a time when the land was teeming with plants and insects.

Caytonia

Pronounced: Kay-*tone*-ee-ah
Lived: 183–100 MYA (Jurassic to Cretaceous)
Size: Shrubs and trees of uncertain height

Caytonia seems to have grown woody stems with leaves sprouting from them. Some scientists believe that it may be a long-lost relative of the flowering plants, because its seeds are covered in a fleshy coating. Like the Bennettitales, *Caytonia* was to die out by the late Cretaceous.

Fossils of *Caytonia* seeds have been found all over the world.

Bennettitales

Pronounced: Benn-ett-eye-*tahl*-eez
Lived: 304–28 MYA (Carboniferous to Paleogene)
Size: up to several yards tall

This name describes a beautiful group of palm-like seed plants that first appeared in the Triassic—a time of violent volcanic eruptions and climate change. Many of them had fat, branching, woody trunks and leaves like those of modern cycads. They produced cone-like structures that may have been visited by insects.

Umaltolepis

Pronounced: Oom-al-to-*lep*-iss
Lived: 125–100 MYA (Cretaceous)
Size: not fully known; shoots to 1.5 in

This fossil tree provided a crucial clue in working out how seed plants evolved. Its leaves are similar to those of *Ginkgo*— a majestic tree that you can still see today. Although *Umaltolepis* had leaves like those of *Gingko* (see page 32), its umbrella-like seed-bearing structures containing winged seeds, were unique.

TAKING OVER

The seed enabled plants to conquer new territory. Seed plants were perfectly suited to the drier habitats where earlier plants just couldn't survive. There was no stopping them now! The fossil plants on these pages belong to a group called the gymnosperms—plants that do not flower, but produce seeds.

Callistophyton

Pronounced: Kall-is-to-*phyte*-on
Lived: 314–306 MYA (Carboniferous)
Size: leaves 12 in long

While looking up at the towering trees in the prehistoric forest, you might have tripped over this shrubby forest floor creeper. Its fat stems were about as thick as your thumb, and its leaves were rather feathery and fern-like. On the underside of the leaves there were orange clusters that looked like spores, but in fact they were producing pollen.

Eremopteris

Pronounced: Er-em-*opt*-ter-is
Lived: 360–272 MYA (Devonian to Permian)
Size: under 3 ft tall; leaves to about 8 in

The next plant on our tour through the swampy fossil forest is *Eremopteris*. It was probably a cousin of *Callistophyton*, but this plant had much smaller leaves—less than the length of your arm. Look out for some of the many monstrous amphibians that are slithering in and out of these plants—some of them are the size of crocodiles!

Glossopterids

Pronounced: Gloss-**opt**-terr-ids
Lived: 300–255 MYA
(Carboniferous to Permian)
Size: up to 98 ft tall

Glossopterid is a name that
describes a group of fossil trees
from which leaves have been found
in far-flung places around the
world. This provides evidence that
the continents drifted apart over
a long period of time. The tongue-
shaped leaves of the glossopterids
could reach the length of a
cucumber, and they sprouted from
the branches of fairly large trees.

Cordaites

Pronounced: Kord-ite-eez
Lived: 383–237 MYA
(Devonian to Triassic)
Size: up to 150 ft

Boots on—we're now on the hunt
for a handsome tree that likes the
water! *Cordaites* grew in a range of
wet habitats, including mangrove-
like swamps, where it poked out
of the seawater, and the edges of
vast tropical wetlands, as well as
drier habitats. It may have looked
a little like the "dragon tree" that
is grown as a popular houseplant.
Cordaites is thought to be a
relative of the conifers that we
will discover later on.

Medullosales

Pronounced: Med-ull-oh-**sahl**-eez
Lived: 360–250 MYA (Devonian
to Triassic)
Size: leaves up to 23 ft

These beautiful fern-like little
trees once dominated the land.
Fossils of Medullosales are found
all across the world. Some species
in the group had seeds about an
inch long, while others had leaves
stretching to 23 ft! The main trunk
was made up of soft pith—
a new form of "plumbing system"
that allowed these plants to grow
strong stems without the need for
lots of wood.

WHEN SEED PLANTS SPREAD

We've just explored some of the first seed plants, such as the seed ferns. Some of them were forerunners of the gymnosperms—a group of plants that produce cones and seeds. Now we're going to take a closer look at some of the gymnosperms that are alive today.

Gnetophytes

Gymnosperms are divided into groups based on their relatedness. Most of the plants on these pages belong to the gnetophytes. Gnetophytes can look very different from each other, but they each contain a special type of water-transport system that is similar to that of the flowering plants.

Ginkgo

Pronounced: *Ging*-koh
Lived: 252 MYA–present (Permian to today)
Size: 50–100 ft

Often called the maidenhair tree, the ginkgo is one of another group of gymnosperms called the gingkophytes. The group dates back 252 million years, but all the other species are now extinct. Although the gingko is native to China, it has been planted all over the world, and is common in parks and gardens. It is a slender tree with beautiful fan-shaped leaves that turn golden in autumn. Can you find one growing near you? If so, you'll be looking at a form of plant that existed long before dinosaurs roamed the Earth.

Welwitschia

Pronounced: Well-*witt*-skee-ah
Lived: alive today
Size: 5 ft

This peculiar plant can survive for over 1,000 years! In all this time, it only produces two leaves. These grow very slowly from the base of the plant and can reach about 46 feet in length, becoming worn and frayed over time. Colonies of *Welwitschia* look like strange sea creatures stranded on the sand.

Welwitschia lives in dry African deserts, where it survives by catching moisture from dew and fog.

Gnetum

Pronounced: *Neet*-uhm
Lived: alive today
Size: to about 50 ft high

Gnetum is a group of about 40 tropical trees and climbers. Unlike most of the other gymnosperms, *Gnetum* produces a sugary syrup to attract pollinating insects, similar to the way flowers do. Before scientists could study their DNA, they believed that gnetophytes like *Gnetum* were the closest relatives of the flowering plants.

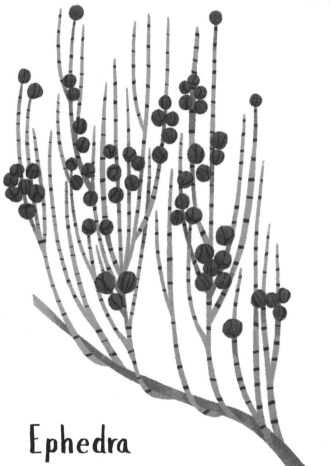

Ephedra

Pronounced: Eff-*ed*-rah
Lived: alive today
Size: up to 6.5 ft

This shrubby plant grows in deserts and other dry habitats, such as on sea cliffs. Its leaves are tiny and scale-like, and fall soon after they are produced. Some species of *Ephedra* are pollinated by wind, and others by insects. The plant has been used for centuries to make herbal medicines.

Eamesia

Pronounced: Eem-*eez*-ee-ah
Lived: 145 MYA (Cretaceous)
Size: 3.5 in tall

We're going back in time to hunt for a fossil gnetophyte, to see what it can tell us about how the group evolved. *Eamesia* is a small shrub that looks similar to modern-day *Ephedra*. But when scientists studied it more closely, they noticed that its male cones were arranged loosely. Its modern relatives have male cones that are closer together. This change may have happened as a result of its habitat drying out.

CYCAD SURVIVORS

Cycads look like palms, but in fact they belong to a very ancient group of non-flowering seed plants. Most have a thick, woody trunk and a crown of stiff, fern-like leaves. They grow very slowly and some specimens may be over 1,000 years old. These incredible plants have survived hungry dinosaurs, ice ages, and asteroids, but many of those that remain today are threatened with extinction.

USING CYCADS

Some cycads, such as *Cycas revoluta*, have become popular pot plants. Others have been put to use in different ways. Pith from the trunk of *Encephalartos* was once cut out and eaten, giving it the nickname "bread tree." People have also soaked, baked, and eaten the seeds of *Macrozamia*. Meanwhile, the long, branched leaves of *Bowenia* are popular for making wreaths.

Ceratozamia

Pronounced: Serr-at-oh-*zame*-ee-ah
Lived: alive today
Size: leaves to 10 ft

The 20 or 30 species in this genus grow in moist mountain forests, especially around Mexico. Part of its name comes from the Greek for "horned," referring to the spiky scales that grow on the plants' cones. The plants have glossy green palm-like leaves with stiff, narrow leaflets. Most species are classified as vulnerable, endangered, or critically endangered in the wild.

Cycas

Pronounced: *Sie*-kass
Lived: alive today
Size: 3–10 ft

Known as the sago palm, *Cycas revoluta* has a cylindrical trunk covered in diamond-shaped markings left by fallen leaves. Its green leaves are leathery and shiny, and just as in other cycads, the male and female parts grow on separate plants.

Encephalartos

Pronounced: Enk-eff-al-*ah*-toss
Lived: alive today
Size: up to about 20 ft

This type of cycad is native to Africa. A specimen of one species, the Eastern Cape giant cycad, was collected by a plant hunter and taken to Kew Gardens in London in 1755. It is still alive and considered to be the world's oldest potted plant.

Some species of *Encephalartos* are called bread palms because a bread-like starchy food can be made from the center of their stems.

Macrozamia

Pronounced: Mac-ro-*zame*-ee-ah
Lived: alive today
Size: larger species up to 30 ft

Macrozamia is a group of about 40 cycads, all of which are native to Australia. Some form stout trees and produce pineapple-like cones. The male and female cones are produced on different plants, and are attractive to a range of pollinators, including beetles, weevils, and tiny insects called thrips. In some cases, the thrips can breed nowhere else and rely on the cycads for their survival.

Bowenia

Pronounced: Bow-*enn*-ee-ah
Lived: alive today
Size: up to about 6.5 ft

This group includes three living species as well as two fossils, all of which come from Australia. The living species grow in the tropical rainforests of Queensland, often close to streams or in groups among grasses and shrubs. Their leaves are branched more than those of the other cycads, and have large, leathery leaflets. The name *Bowenia* honors the first governor of Queensland, Sir George Ferguson Bowen.

WHEN CONIFERS CONQUERED

Seeds were so successful that by 240 million years ago, seed-producing gymnosperms dominated the land. The earliest species had seeds that helicoptered to the ground, keeping them afloat for longer. This allowed them to travel long distances before sprouting.

Meet the family

Around the world, there are still about 1,000 different species of gymnosperms alive today, divided into four main groups. We've already explored three of them: the bizarre gnetophytes, the sole surviving ginkgophyte, and the cycads. Now it's time to look at the fourth group: the conifers.

Thucydia

Pronounced: Thoo-*side*-ee-ah
Lived: 303–299 MYA (Carboniferous)
Size: probably up to about 6.5 ft

Conifer forests still dominate much of our planet today. But first, let's hop back 300 million years to the fossil forests where their ancestors grew. *Thucydia* looks like a miniature version of an *Araucaria*—better known as the monkey puzzle tree. Some of the colossal modern conifers may have evolved from something much smaller, like *Thucydia*.

Voltziales

Pronounced: Volt-zee-*ah*-leez
Lived: 280–209 MYA (Permian to Triassic)
Size: variable; some were tall trees

Walking along the fossil forest track, you'll see extinct conifers belonging to a group called the Voltziales. At a time when many other plants became extinct, these tough conifers managed to survive. One member of the group, called *Walchia*, had a long bare trunk without branches and leaves. The Voltziales may have been the link between *Cordaites* (see page 31) and the modern conifer families.

Wollemia

Pronounced: Woll-*ehm*-ee-ah
Lived: alive today
Size: up to 89 ft

Until 1994, this type of conifer was known only from fossils. Then a living population was found in a remote rainforest in the Wollemi National Park in Australia, just 93 miles from Sydney. To find a plant that was thought to have died out with the dinosaurs so close to human civilization was an extraordinary discovery.

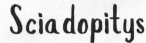

The Wollemi pine is grown in botanical gardens all over the world.

Metasequoia

Pronounced: Met-a-seck-*quoy*-ah
Lived: alive today
Size: 164 ft

About 45 million years ago, this majestic tree dominated the land north of the Arctic Circle. Scientists thought it was extinct until the 1940s, when a new species of *Metasequoia* was discovered growing in China. The living species is a fast-growing plant known as the "dawn redwood." Unlike many other conifers, it loses its leaves in winter.

Sciadopitys

Pronounced: Sie-ah-*dop*-It-Iss
Lived: alive today
Size: up to 89 ft

This special tree is one of a kind—like the dawn redwood, it has no close living ancestors. It has existed for about 230 million years, and *Sciadopitys* forests were once widespread across the Northern Hemisphere. This "living fossil" now grows wild in Japan, and what appear to be leaves are in fact modified stems—special structures called cladodes. *Sciadopitys* produces seeds in scaly brown cones.

COLOSSAL CONIFERS

Conifers have survived a lot, from drifting continents, changing climates, and erupting volcanoes to the rise of flowering plants. These venerable giants have existed on our planet for at least 300 million years, and are among the oldest living seed plants alive. Today they cover vast tracts of land in North America and Eurasia, especially in mountain forests.

Sequoiadendron

Pronounced: Seck-quoy-ah-*den*-dron
Lived: alive today
Size: up to 310 ft tall

Here is another giant of our time. Known as the giant sequoia, its height and wide trunk make it one of the most massive trees on Earth. It is native to the mountains of California, where its fire-resistant bark protects it from small, frequent fires. In fact, the ashes left by the fires are perfect for seedlings to establish in.

Sequoia

Pronounced: Seck-*quoy*-ah
Lived: alive today
Size: up to 377 ft tall

This extraordinary tree, also called the coast redwood, grows in the moist coastal forests of California, where it reaches heights of up to 377 feet. Although fast-growing, these trees may take centuries to reach maturity. They are also among the oldest living organisms, reaching an age of up to about 2,000 years.

RECORD-BREAKERS

Today's conifers include some amazing record-breakers. One coastal redwood, a tree called "Hyperion," is the tallest living organism on Earth. And a specimen of the giant sequoia, the "General Sherman," has a trunk spanning 36 feet—wider than a London bus is long! And one bristlecone pine has reached the astonishing age of over 4,800 years, making it one of the oldest living organisms.

Araucaria

Pronounced: A-rau-*kah*-ree-ah
Lived: alive today
Size: 130 ft

The curiously beautiful monkey puzzle tree is endangered in the wild. It grows in the moist temperate rainforests of south-central Chile and Argentina. In Chile, its distribution is divided between the Andes and the coast. The tree's edible seeds, known as *piñones*, are eaten by the indigenous Pehuenche people of Chile.

Pinus longaeva

Pronounced: Pine-uhss long-*gyve*-ah
Lived: alive today
Size: 50 ft high

We've gazed up at the largest trees on Earth—now let's look at the oldest! Known as the bristlecone pine, this conifer grows in cold, dry mountain slopes in the western United States. Its gnarled, twisted trunk can remain standing centuries after the tree eventually dies.

Methuselah, the world's oldest bristlecone pine, is kept a closely-guarded secret, to protect it from vandals.

Today, drugs used to treat people with cancer are extracted from this tree.

Taxus

Pronounced: *Tacks*-uhss
Lived: alive today
Size: 33–66 ft

Better known as the yew tree, this conifer forms an important part of European history and folklore. The species *Taxus baccata* can live for hundreds or even thousands of years. It has scaly, brown bark and flat, narrow leaves, and nearly all parts of the tree are poisonous. Ancient yews are common around old buildings where they may have been planted in the belief that they offered protection.

WHEN FLOWERS FORMED

Eventually the thriving forests of gymnosperms had to compete with a new type of plant altogether. Let's go back to the Cretaceous period—or possibly even earlier—when dinosaurs were prowling the primeval forests. Something extraordinary is about to happen: the first flowering plants are evolving. They became so successful that they changed the face of our planet forever.

Montsechia

Pronounced: Mont-*seck*-ee-ah
Lived: 130-125 MYA (Cretaceous)
Size: branches about 4 in long

How did the first flowering plants fill the various habitats that were available to them? Some scientists thought that they grew in dark forests, while others suggested that they grew in or near water. When scientists re-examined fossils of *Montsechia* in 2015, they discovered that the plant lacks roots and lived underwater, like a pondweed. Perhaps some of the world's very first flowers unfurled underwater!

Nanjinganthus

Pronounced: Nan-jing-*ganth*-uhss
Lived: 174 MYA (Jurassic)
Size: flowers about ½ in across

Fossils of this mysterious plant were discovered in an area of China well known for being rich in fossils from the Early Jurassic, when swimming reptiles ruled the waves. Examining the fossils under the microscope, scientists rebuilt an image to show how the plant might have looked. But they still disagree over whether *Nanjinganthus* was even a flowering plant at all.

THE FIRST FLOWER!

Even though the dinosaurs have been extinct for 66 million years, we have a better idea of what they looked like than we do the first flowers. This is because although there are some fossils of these early plants, most were fragile and didn't preserve well. But by piecing together evidence from the few fossils there are, alongside the many flowers that are alive today, scientists have rebuilt an image of what the very first flowers could have looked like. They think that these early blooms may have looked rather like a magnolia.

Juraherba

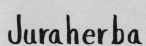

Pronounced: Jur-ah-**herb**-ah
Lived: 164 MYA (Jurassic)
Size: up to 1.5 in

Here is another botanical mystery, a tiny fossil plant dug up in northern China. *Juraherba* may have grown in lakes surrounded by moist, warm forests of giant conifers, ginkgos, and cycads. It had thin leaves, almost like grasses, and what appear to be bursting fruits containing seeds—an important feature of the flowering plants. Based on a single fossil, it is difficult to know for certain whether *Juraherba* was truly a flowering plant. But it is a valuable piece in the complicated jigsaw of plant evolution.

Archaefructus

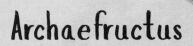

Pronounced: Ark-ee-**fruct**-uhss
Lived: 130–125 MYA (Cretaceous)
Size: branches about 4 in long

Keep the waders on, because now we're going to hunt down another pondweed that grows in shallow lakes shared by dinosaurs and other prehistoric creatures. Fossils of this ancient flower were discovered in a slab of stone in northeast China. Pondweeds like *Archaefructus* and *Montsechia* may not look very impressive, but they may be the ancestors of all flowering plants we see today—and that makes them very special.

WHEN FLOWERS FLOURISHED

The famous naturalist Charles Darwin described the sudden appearance of flowers in the fossil record—flowers that resembled those we see today—as an "abominable mystery." And over a century later, the puzzle of how the first flowers evolved still has scientists scratching their heads.

A world in bloom

But what is set in stone is that once flowers got going, there was just no stopping them! Go back 100 million years, and all sorts of new plants were flourishing. They took many forms, from woody plants like the laurels and sycamores we see today, to roses and water lilies.

Archaeanthus

Pronounced: Ark-ee-*anth*-uhss
Lived: 100 MYA (Cretaceous)
Size: fruiting structure up to 6 in

Fossil fruits are often much better preserved than flowers, because they were less fragile. This means that scientists can tell that the fruiting head of *Archaeanthus* would have had up to 300 tightly packed structures, each with nearly 100 seeds inside. These structures have scars that mark where the flowers grew.

Destined for success

By the middle of the Cretaceous period, many different land habitats became dominated by flowering plants. The fleshy leaves, soft flowers, and juicy fruits of the early species must have been a tasty snack for the animals of the time. Dinosaurs ate gymnosperms too, but perhaps the flowering plants were better at growing back quickly.

Lesqueria

Pronounced: Lesk-*eer*-ree-ah
Lived: 100 MYA (Cretaceous)
Size: fruiting structure less than 4 in

Like *Archaeanthus*, this fossil shrub probably had flowers a little like those of a magnolia, and fruits with hundreds of seeds. Below the fruiting structure were many leafy, diamond-shaped flaps. This peculiar plant grew at a time when dinosaurs called ornithopods darted through the forest, flying reptiles called pterosaurs soared across the sky, and plesiosaurs swam the seas.

Prisca

Pronounced: *Priss*-kah
Lived: 100 MYA (Cretaceous)
Size: fruiting catkins about 2.75 in long

Fossils of this unusual woody plant have been found in Kansas, USA. It probably grew along the wet banks of lagoons. It was a shrub or small tree with seeds that were most likely spread by wind and water, and grew in long, hanging catkins.

Paleoclusia

Pronounced: Pale-ee-oh-*kloos*-ee-ah
Lived: 95 MYA (Cretaceous)
Size: flowers less than 1/16 in

This fossil flower was just a couple of millimeters across, but it had a big impact on the botanical world. It is an ancestor of the Clusiaceae, a modern family of tropical trees and shrubs. *Paleoclusia* had five petals and bunches of pollen-producing stamens. But we still do not know what the leafy part of the plant looked like.

Scandianthus

Pronounced: Scand-ee-*anth*-uhss
Lived: 85 MYA (Cretaceous)
Size: flowers 1/16 in

All sorts of interesting new plants were evolving, and the fossil record is crammed full of flowers like *Scandianthus*. It had five petals and produced nectar to entice insects. *Scandianthus* was probably similar to modern flowers called saxifrages.

PECULiAR PALEO PLANTS

Scientists have shown that the first group to branch off in the flowering plant family tree is made up of just a few hundred, very ancient living species. These include the water lilies, along with the woody, often aromatic plants found on these pages. These peculiar "paleo plants" are called basal angiosperms and they hold important clues that help us to understand how the flowering plants became so dominant.

Amborella

Pronounced: Am-bor-*rell*-ah
Lived: alive today
Size: up to 26 ft

This shrub grows only on the Pacific island of New Caledonia, where conditions have changed very little for millions of years. *Amborella* has crinkly-edged leaves, cream-colored flowers, and little, red berry-like fruits. This rather ordinary-looking plant may hold clues about how flowers first appeared. About 130 million years ago, its ancestor split off from all the other flowering plants in the family tree that are alive today.

SPICES AND MEDICINES
A species of *Illicium*, known as star anise, is used to flavor food and drink. It is also used in traditional medicine across Asia, and it produces a chemical that is used to make medication to treat influenza. *Schisandra* also has a long history of use in Traditional Chinese Medicine.

Illicium

Pronounced: Ill-*ih*-see-uhm
Lived: alive today
Size: 26–50 ft

Many species in this group of trees and shrubs from the shady forests of eastern Asia and North America have peculiar flowers with long petals twisting outward. They produce star-like fruits with 6–8 boat-shaped sections that shoot out their seeds explosively.

Schisandra

Pronounced: Shiss-*ahnd*-rah
Lived: alive today
Size: vines to several yards

This climbing plant is native to the warm temperate and subtropical forests of Asia and North America. It is sometimes called a "magnolia vine," although it is not a true magnolia. The scarlet, salty-tasting berries of *Schisandra* are eaten by birds that disperse the plant's seeds.

Kadsura

Pronounced: Kad-*sue*-rah
Lived: alive today
Size: up to 16.5 ft

This twining shrub grows in the warm wet woods in Asia. Some varieties are grown for their extraordinary scarlet fruits that grow to the size of small soccer balls! The plant has shiny green leaves and beautiful cup-shaped flowers that can be green, yellow, white, or red.

Working together

In some species of *Kadsura*, the flowers attract midges that lay their eggs on them. Laying the eggs triggers the plant to produce a sticky resin that feeds the growing midge larvae. In return for providing the midges with a nursery, the insects pollinate the plant's flowers.

Austrobaileya

Pronounced: Os-tro-*bale*-ee-yah
Lived: alive today
Size: up to 50 ft

To see this rare, woody creeper, you need to trek through the understorey of Australia's tropical rainforests. Here, you will find it winding its stems around tall trees, twisting its way up to the canopy, where it sends out pairs of leathery blue-green leaves. Its pale greenish-yellow flowers are covered in tiny purple dots, and they produce a rotten smell that attracts flies. The orange fruits are pear-shaped.

WATER LiLY WiLDERNESS

Ready to dive back in? Water lilies are another group of very ancient plants that long ago branched off the flowering plant family tree. Leaves and flowers like those on these pages may have been floating in watery wildernesses around the world for almost 100 million years. Isn't that incredible?

Life afloat

These beautiful plants are aquatic, meaning that they live in ponds, lakes and rivers. They survive in these habitats by anchoring their roots in the soft mud at the bottom. Their leaves and flowers float on the surface of the water to capture sunlight and attract pollinators.

Microvictoria

Pronounced: My-**cro**-vic-tor-ee-a
Lived: 113–98 MYA (Cretaceous)
Size: flowers 3.5 mm long

This extinct water lily had flowers that could fit on your little fingernail! The flowers may have been pollinated by tiny beetles that were attracted by the flowers' perfume. These beetles may then have become trapped and showered with pollen, much like the pollinators of its giant descendants, which grow in the Amazon today.

> The leaves of *Victoria* are so strong they can support the weight of a small child!

Victoria

Pronounced: Vic-**tor**-ee-a
Lived: alive today
Size: leaves to nearly 3 m across

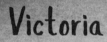

Known as the giant Amazonian water lily, this is perhaps one of the most astonishing and beautiful of all plants. Its leaves form vast carpets of gigantic floating discs on the surface of pools in South America. The rim around the leaf is upturned, but has a slit that acts as a drain during tropical rainstorms. Even its flowers are extraordinary! They are white when they open, and attract beetles that become trapped in the flowers overnight. The following day, they turn pink and the beetles are released.

Euryale

Pronounced: You-*rahl*-ee
Lived: alive today
Size: leaves to about 3 ft across

Gloves on—this cousin of the giant Amazonian water lily is sometimes called the prickly water lily, and for good reason! It grows in low-lying pools across Asia, and its leaves can stretch to nearly 3 feet across. They are round and crinkly, and if you turn one over, you would see that the underside is a vivid purple color.

Nymphaea

Pronounced: *Nimf*-ee-yah
Lived: alive today
Size: leaves about 8 in across

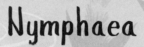

Numphaea flowers can be found in ornamental gardens all over the world.

This group of water lilies has breathtakingly beautiful flowers that come in a whole kaleidoscope of colors ranging from white to pink, to mauve and purple. The fruits mature under the surface of the water.

SAILING SEEDS

Seeds may have a better chance of success if they sprout farther from their parent plant. Some get away by floating! The seeds of *Nuphar* and *Nymphaea* have a layer of slime that traps air bubbles, allowing them to float away. When the bubbly rafts rot away, the seeds sink to the muddy bed to germinate.

Nuphar

Pronounced: *Nufe*-ar
Lived: alive today
Size: leaves about 8 in across

This group of water lilies grows in ponds, lakes, and rivers across the Northern Hemisphere. Their flowers have 4–6 petals that poke above the water's surface. Those of some species attract flies, while others produce a fragrance that beetles find irresistible.

MAGNIFICENT MAGNOLIAS

The very first flowers may have looked something like a magnolia. Now we're going to look more closely at this very ancient group of plants, and its close relatives—a group that is called the Magnoliales. It contains many fascinating plants besides magnolias—from custard apples to tulip trees, and even nutmeg!

Futabanthus

Pronounced: Foo-ta-*banth*-uhss
Lived: 90 MYA (Cretaceous)
Size: flowers less than ½ in across

The discovery of this fossil flower in Japan showed that the custard apple family evolved earlier than scientists had previously thought. The small flower had whorls of petal-like structures and a disc, about 1/8 inch across. This plant was alive at a time when enormous, long-necked dinosaurs called sauropods lumbered across the land.

Annona

Pronounced: An-*own*-ah
Lived: alive today
Size: fruit to 4 in across

You may recognize this living descendent of plants like *Futabanthus*—it is called the custard apple, or sugar apple. Its fruit is about the size of a small tennis ball. Inside the thick rind of knobbly segments is a sweet-smelling creamy white flesh with shiny dark seeds. Custard apples may have been grown for food for thousands of years, but their ancestors go back much further than this.

Liriodendron

Pronounced: Lee-ree-oh-*den*-dron
Lived: alive today
Size: trees up to about 200 ft

This glorious plant is often called the tulip tree because of its large, tulip-like flowers. Fossils show that trees like these were around at about the same time as *Futabanthus*, making *Liriodendron* another example of a "living fossil" plant. Today there are two species—one native to North America and the other to Asia. The flowers have greenish sepals (the outermost parts) and orange-flushed petals.

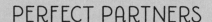

PERFECT PARTNERS

The beautiful flowers of some of the plants in this group, such as *Myristica* and *Magnolia*, are often pollinated by beetles—just as they probably were tens of millions of years ago. In fact, some fruity-smelling magnolia flowers are large enough to hold several beetles at a time! The custard apple's peculiar yellowish flowers are pollinated by equally unusual-looking insects called rhinoceros beetles.

Southern Magnolia

Myristica

Pronounced: Meer-riss-*steek*-er
Lived: alive today
Size: tree to 50 ft

Nutmeg is an evergreen tree native to Indonesia where it is an important crop. Its seeds have long been used for medicine and as a spice or preservative for food. Mace is the lacy red structure (scientifically known as an aril) that forms a casing around the shiny seed, and splits open when ripe. Mace is also used for flavoring food.

Magnolia

Pronounced: Mag-*nole*-ee-yah
Lived: alive today
Size: variable; shrubs to trees several yards high

Magnolia seeds collected from 2,000-year-old tombs have been grown successfully!

Today there are 200 or so of these very beautiful and ancient plants which are widespread around the world, especially in Asia. Fossils show that plants remarkably similar to those alive today grew tens of millions of years ago. Some magnolias have extraordinary-looking fruits, like the one shown (*Magnolia zenii*).

BIZARRE BIRTHWORTS

This ancient family is known scientifically as the Aristolochiaceae, but that's quite a mouthful! Plants in this family are often called birthworts, and they produce some of the most bizarre flowers you will see anywhere. There are about 500 species, many of which are tropical vines and creepers.

Aristolochia grandiflora

Pronounced: Ar-is-tol-lock-ee-ya grand-ih-*floor*-rah
Lived: alive today
Size: flowers up to 24 in long

This vine grows in tropical thickets in the Caribbean and Central America. The name *grandiflora* means "large flower," and this plant's trumpet-shaped flowers reach a length of 24 inches! The green and red flowers, which give off an unpleasant scent that attracts flies, last for just two days.

PECULIAR POLLINATION

Many birthwort flowers attract small flying insects that crawl down a funnel. The funnel is lined with downward-pointing hairs that are easy to slide down, but difficult to crawl up again, leaving the insects trapped in the flower overnight. The next day, the hairs wither, unblocking the flower's escape passage. The pollen-laden insects fly away, carrying pollen to other birthwort flowers.

To our eyes these flowers look just like the face of Darth Vader!

Aristolochia salvadorensis

Pronounced: Ar-is-tol-*lock*-ee-ya sal-va-door-*ren*-siss
Lived: alive today
Size: flowers about 2 in

Like the other birthworts, the flower has no petals. But it does smell just like the fungi that decompose in rotting wood and plant material. This tricks weak-flying little insects—the larvae of which feed on the fungi—into the flower to pollinate it. Now that's a "rotten" trick!

What's in a name?

It was once believed that the *Aristolochia clematitis* could speed up childbirth, because the shape of its tubular yellow flowers was thought to resemble the outline of a uterus. In fact, the plant had no such effect, but this is how the birthworts earned their name.

Aristolochia clematitis

Pronounced: Ar-is-tol-*lock*-ee-ya clem-*aht*-it-iss
Lived: alive today
Size: flowers about 2.5 in

This plant is often found sprawling around ancient buildings, such as abbeys, where it was grown for herbal medicine. But that was centuries ago, and we now know that the plant is toxic, and should not be eaten.

Aristolochia fimbriata

Pronounced: Ar-is-tol-*lock*-ee-ya fim-bree-*aht*-ah
Lived: alive today
Size: flowers about 2 in

Like *Aristolochia salvadorensis*, this bizarre birthwort is also native to South America. It scrambles over the vegetation, sending forth fabulously unique flowers. The flowers appear from the base of the leaf stalks, and each one has a whitish-green pouch and tube, flared at the top and fringed with curly white tentacles.

Aristolochia ridicula

Pronounced: Aristol-*lock*-ee-ya rid-*ihc*-culah
Lived: Alive today
Size: flowers 2.5 in

This extraordinary birthwort is native to the tropical forests and leafy thickets of Brazil and Bolivia. If the other birthworts' flowers on this page look peculiar, those of this plant are downright bizarre—they could even be described as looking ridiculous, hence its name! It has a blotchy purple inflated tube, and two extended, backward-pointing horn-like structures that resemble an insect's antennae, covered in little tentacles (called trichomes). It is a truly astonishing flower!

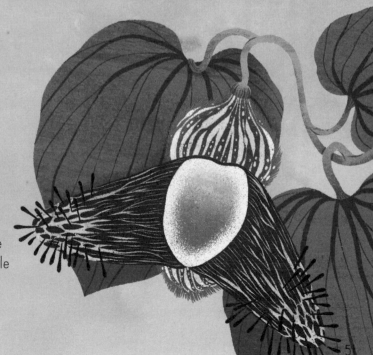

A MULTITUDE OF MONOCOTS

The monocots are one of the two major groups of flowering plants, and probably evolved early in their history. Some monocots are very familiar, while others are downright bizarre. It's time to take a look at some of the monocots you don't see every day!

What's a monocot?

Monocots typically have leaves with parallel veins, and flowers arranged in threes. They include the grasses, bulbs, and orchids. Many monocots—particularly the grasses—are widespread as food crops. Do you eat rice, wheat, or maize? These are all monocots. Other food plants, such as ginger and pineapple, are monocots too.

FEASTING ON FUNGUS

Most plants contain a green substance called chlorophyll that allows them to make food using sunlight. But *Mabelia*, *Thismia*, and their close relatives don't have chlorophyll, so they can't make their own food. Instead, they survive by stealing their nutrients from fungi.

Arisaema

Pronounced: Ar-iss-*eem*-ah
Lived: alive today
Size: flowering structures 8 in

Just when you thought flowers couldn't get any weirder... along comes the aroid family! Several thousand different species grow throughout the world, especially in the rainforests. Their unique flowering structures are made up of a spike-like structure called a spadix, and a leafy spathe. Some plants in this group produce heat, which is attractive to pollinating insects.

Mabelia

Pronounced: Mah-*bell*-ee-yah
Lived: 90 MYA (Cretaceous)
Size: 1/8 in across

This unusual fossil flower was discovered in New Jersey, USA. It is one of the oldest monocot flowers, dating back to the late Cretaceous. The flowers of *Mabelia* were tiny, with 6 petal-like structures. Scientists believe that the plant belongs to a strange family called Triuridaceae.

Etlingera

Pronounced: Et-*linj*-eh-rah
Lived: alive today
Size: flowering shoots up to 5 ft high

This group of plants grow in the tropics across Asia and Australia. Like its relative the ginger plant, *Etlingera* produces creeping underground stems called rhizomes. Some species produce tall shoots up to 33 feet high, while others grow in clumps. The species shown here is often called the "torch flower." Its waxy red flower clusters can bloom for several months.

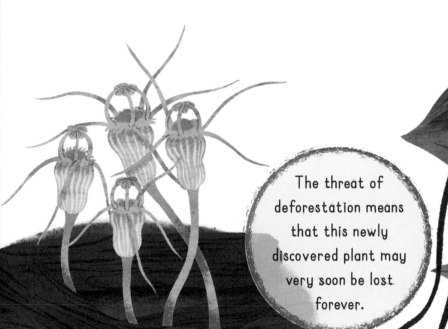

The threat of deforestation means that this newly discovered plant may very soon be lost forever.

Thismia

Pronounced: *Thiz*-mee-yah
Lived: alive today
Size: flowers 1.25 in

Could you imagine a stranger flower than this? *Thismia* is a group of extraordinary monocots from the tropics that scarcely even resemble plants at all. The species shown here is called a "fairy lantern," and it was found very recently in the rainforests of Borneo.

Tacca

Pronounced: *Tack*-ah
Lived: alive today
Size: flower stalks 20 in high

This unusual plant is known as the "bat flower," and it is not hard to see why! It is actually a distant relative of the yam—an edible root vegetable that is an important source of food in the tropics. There are about 15 species of *Tacca*, most of which grow in the forests of Southeast Asia.

EXTRAORDINARY ORCHIDS

The orchids make up one of the largest of all plant families, with about 30,000 species. Many of them have evolved bizarre relationships with pollinating insects such as bees, wasps, flies, and moths. Flowers often produce sugary nectar to attract pollinators, but many orchids use deception instead. Some orchid flowers advertise nectar but have none, while others pretend to be something they are not, fooling insects into visiting and transferring pollen. Orchids are the con artists of the plant world.

Meliorchis

Pronounced: Mell-ee-**ork**-iss
Lived: 20–15 MYA (Miocene)
Size: unknown

There are few orchids in the fossil record, so how they evolved is still poorly understood. When *Meliorchis* pollen was found attached to a small bee trapped in ancient amber, scientists were able to compare it with living orchid species and work out that the first orchids may have evolved 76–84 million years ago.

Angraecum

Pronounced: Ang-**greek**-uhm
Lived: alive today
Size: flower spur up to 16 in

Charles Darwin predicted that the extraordinarily long spur that trails from the flower of this beautiful orchid (*Angraecum sesquipedale*) must be visited by a moth with an equally long tongue. At the time, no such moth had ever been seen. But 21 years after Darwin's death, the moth was discovered, and his prediction was found to be correct! This incredible orchid, along with its moth pollinator, are one of the most celebrated examples of his theory of evolution.

54

Coryanthes

Pronounced: Coh-ree-*anth*-eez
Lived: alive today
Size: flowers 5 in

Like many other orchids, the so-called "bucket orchids" trick their pollinators. Male bees harvest a special perfume produced only by the orchid's flowers, which they use to attract female bees—like an orchid-branded bee body spray! As they collect the scent, the bees often tumble into the flowers' fluid-filled pouches. The bees pollinate the flowers as they emerge from the buckets, bedraggled and bewildered.

Rhizanthella

Pronounced: Rize-*anth*-ell-ah
Lived: alive today
Size: flowerheads about ¾ in across

Orchids are well known for being beautiful and eye-catching, but this one blooms out of sight—underground, in fact! Like its distant relative *Thismia*, it has no chlorophyll and obtains its food from a fungus. In fact, it looks more like a fungus than it does a plant. When the orchid was found in Australia in 1928, no one had ever seen a flower quite like it. Since then, a handful of similar related species have been unearthed across Australia.

There are over 800 species of Habenaria orchid and they grow all over the world.

Habenaria

Pronounced: Hab-en-*ah*-ree-ah
Lived: alive today
Size: flowers 1.5 in

The full name of this beautiful orchid is *Habenaria medusa* and it is native to the forests of Java, Sumatra, Sulawesi, and Borneo in Southeast Asia—an area that is rich in orchids. This particularly unusual one has flowers with a fringe of long white strands, and is attractive to moths.

EUDICOT DOMINANCE

About three-quarters of all flowering plants today are eudicots. They are found in nearly every green habitat! Formerly known as "dicots," these plants usually have net-veined leaves and flowers in multiples of four, five, or seven. They are bewilderingly diverse, ranging from giant oaks to dainty daisies. They also include familiar food plants such as peaches, apples, peas, and sunflowers. But where did this important group first come from? Let's see what's lurking in the fossil record.

Leefructus

Pronounced: Lee-*frook*-tuhss
Lived: 125 MYA (Cretaceous)
Size: flowers ¼ in

This fossil plant from northern China looks tantalizingly similar to some of the most ancient eudicots alive today—members of the buttercup family. It grew at a time of feathered dinosaurs, birds, mammals, and gliding lizards. It had shoots with clusters of 3-lobed leaves.

There are over 100 species of *Protea*, including a truly spectacular one called the king protea.

Dinganthus

Pronounced: Ding-**ganth**-uhss
Lived: 20–15 MYA (Miocene)
Size: flowers 1/7 in

Here is another long-lost eudicot flower that was found recently in a piece of amber in the Dominican Republic. It had 5 petals, as well as 10 pollen-producing stamens. This fossil *Dinganthus* flower provides evidence that flowers evolved from a condensed shoot with parts sprouting from the sides. It also helps botanists to understand the unusual appearance of other fossil flowering plants, such as those of *Archaefructus*.

Lijinganthus

Pronounced: Lih-jing-**ganth**-uhss
Lived: 99 MYA (Cretaceous)
Size: flowers ¼ in

At some point between the Early and Late Cretaceous, the eudicots exploded in diversity. Unlike most fossil flowers, this one, found in Myanmar, is exquisitely complete. It includes all parts of a typical flower and scientists were able to classify it confidently as a eudicot. It has tiny sepals and large, curved petals. The presence of a disc like those that produce nectar in living plants suggests that it may have been pollinated by insects.

Protea

Pronounced: **Prote**-ee-ah
Lived: alive today
Size: flower heads to 12 in across

The proteas belong to an ancient family called the Proteaceae. This family branched off from the rest of the eudicots early on. It has both living and fossil plants found on all the southern continents. The family may have had already divided into two groups before the break-up of the Gondwanaland continent about 140 million years ago. The extraordinary-looking flowers are visited by birds and rodents, as well as insects.

Nelumbo

Pronounced: Nell-**uhm**-bow
Lived: alive today
Size: flowers to 12 in across

Nelumbo seeds found in an ancient lake bed in China that were dated to about 1,300 years old were still able to germinate!

This plant may look like a water lily, but it is actually a eudicot. It is part of an ancient group that—like the proteas—branched off early in the evolution of the other eudicots. This plant is often called the sacred or Indian lotus, and its seeds can survive for incredibly long periods. They may be part of one of the early lotus crops cultivated by Buddhists after the religion was introduced in that part of China.

FLOWERING PLANTS TODAY

We've trekked through fossil forests, swum across prehistoric lakes, and climbed trees. Now we arrive on today's green planet—a place that still teems with plant life, as it has done for millions of years. From the simple seaweeds to unfurling ferns, colossal conifers and beautiful flowers: plants from all these groups—including some of the most ancient—continue to thrive on Earth.

Up to 90% of the plant species we see around us today belong to the flowering plants—a group that, as we have seen, evolved very rapidly. Let's look at a handful of the hundreds of thousands that exist today.

Carnegiea

Pronounced: Karn-*edge*-ee-ah
Lived: alive today
Size: up to 59 ft

This giant cactus is often called the "saguaro," and it towers above the other cacti in the North and Central American deserts. Its roots spread far and wide to absorb rainwater quickly, which it stores in its tall, fat stems. Its flowers open at dusk and are visited by insects, birds, and even bats. Bats make excellent pollinators because their thick fur picks up pollen as they bury their heads in the flowers. Like many cacti, the saguaro has sharp spines that protect it from thirsty desert animals.

Lithops

Pronounced: *Lith*-ops
Lived: alive today
Size: ¾–1.25 in across

It is not hard to see why this plant is known as the "pebble plant" or "living stone." It is a master of camouflage, with a texture and pattern—including mottled stripes, lines, and dots—just like the pebbles and stones that surround it.

Hungry tortoises walk straight over a would-be meal, mistaking the plant for a stone.

Nepenthes

Pronounced: Nep-*enth*-eez
Lived: alive today
Size: pitchers about 8 in long

Often called pitcher plants, most *Nepenthes* trap prey.
Insects tumble into the leafy tubes and drown, releasing
nutrients for the plants. This one, however, has evolved a
special relationship with a species of bat. The bats shelter
from predators in the leafy pitchers, and their droppings
fall to the base of the pitcher. This provides the plant
with a dollop of manure—perfect for helping it survive on
poor soils.

These are tropical
plants that you can
often see growing in
botanical gardens.

Dionaea

Pronounced: Die-*own*-ee-ah
Lived: alive today
Size: traps about ¾ in across

The Venus flytrap evolved traps to capture insects
in environments where nutrients are in short supply.
If an unsuspecting insect crawls onto its leafy jaws,
they snap shut to trap it. As the insect wriggles
inside, digestive juices break it down, releasing
nutrients for the plant. Once the Venus flytrap has
digested its meal, the jaws spring open again, ready
for their next victim.

Huernia

Pronounced: Hoo-*urhn*-ee-yah
Lived: alive today
Size: flowers 2 in

This curious looking plant grows in dry stony habitats
in southern Africa. Like the saguaro cactus and the
lithops, it stores water in its succulent, spiky stems.
The plant shown is a species called *H. zebrina* and its
extraordinary flowers are indeed striped like a zebra!
They also have a raised, shiny red ring called an annulus.
The odd-looking flowers of this plant and its relatives
produce an unpleasant smell. They are attractive to
flies that mistake them for rotting meat and bring
about their pollination. Yum!

PLANTS AND PEOPLE

Why are plants important?

Plants and animals make up the biosphere—the thin layer of life that covers the Earth. We depend on this diversity of life, in all its many forms, for our very existence. For example, plants produce the oxygen we breathe and the food we eat. Plants are also used to make important medicines and clothes. But sadly, the biosphere that we call home has never been in as much danger as it is today.

Extinction: not just a thing of the past

When you hear the word "endangered," perhaps it conjures up thoughts of animals like tigers, pandas, and rhinos. But plants can be endangered too. This means that they are at risk of extinction—becoming lost forever. And without plants, animals cannot survive either.

Extinction has happened throughout Earth's history. In fact, there have been about half a dozen times when huge numbers of species of plants and animals died out in a short period of time—such as at the end of the Cretaceous, when most dinosaurs became extinct. These events are called mass extinctions.

Sadly, we are currently in the middle of another mass extinction. But unlike previous mass extinctions, it is not the result of an asteroid or volcanic activity. This one is being caused by humans.

Plants in danger

In parts of South America, Africa, and Asia, thick rainforests provide a home for many different plants and animals. But large areas of rainforest have been cut down to make way for growing crops to feed our growing population. Meanwhile, rare plants, such as orchids, are collected from their native habitats and sold online around the world. And our inter-connected world means that plants can now spread from one continent to another, where they take over new areas, forcing out native species. This all means that two in five of the world's plant species are now at risk of extinction. If we want to survive, we must protect plants and their habitats, all around the world.

PLANT SAFARI

You don't need to go back in time or trek to a tropical rainforest to see fascinating plants. They are growing all around us! Next time you leave your house, look at the incredible diversity of plants all around you. Each one tells a story.

High and low

Many local parks contain living fossils in the form of conifers. A stroll down your street can be a glimpse back even further, into the Permian: ginkgos are often planted on roadsides and these trees date back 270 million years! Remember to look down as well as up, to find miniature forests of mosses and liverworts at your feet. They are relatives of the very first plants to have conquered the land some 470 million years ago.

Plant a fossil forest!

Why not plant your own prehistoric forest? You can grow plants that ruled the Earth long before the first dinosaurs on your windowsill!

What to do:
1. Collect a handful of moss—look in the moist, shady places in a yard. But don't take moss from a wild habitat (such as a forest) and make sure you ask for permission if you're collecting it from someone else's yard.

2. Wash the moss carefully with rainwater, or with water that has been boiled and left to cool.

3. Find a clean glass container such as a large jam jar and fill the bottom few centimeters with a layer of clean pebbles or marbles.

4. Add a thin layer of potting compost and place the moss you have collected on top.

5. Put the lid on the jar and place it in a light position out of direct sunlight, such as a north-facing windowsill. Then watch your magical moss forest grow!

Plant a tree for the future

The trees you see growing around you all started as tiny seeds, many years ago. Just as you enjoy trees planted by people long ago, you can plant your own tree that others will enjoy in years to come. Isn't that amazing?

Here's what you need to do:
1. Find a few tree seeds. There will be lots lying on the ground in the autumn. Acorns, conkers, and sweet chestnuts should be easy to find.

2. Plant three of the seeds in a large pot full of compost. Push the seeds down to the depth of your little finger.

3. Keep the pot damp and check for signs of growth in the spring. If all three sprout, weed out the weaker two to leave one strong seedling.

4. Once the sapling is as long as your arm, it is time to plant it in the ground. With an adult, find a space where the tree will have plenty of room. You will need to water it often in its first year after planting!

Pressed for time?

Cut plants will wilt and eventually rot. Botanists (scientists who study plants) preserve specimens by pressing and drying them. The specimens are stored in vast collections called herbaria, which keep a record of which plants were growing in a given place and time.

Why not press your own specimen? Find a leaf or flower and place it on a piece of board or thick paper. Cover with a piece of paper, then place something heavy and flat on top, like a large book. After 3–4 weeks, your leaf should be completely dry and ready to mount.

Create a seed bank

Banks save money for the future. A seed bank saves plants for the future! Seeds from many different plants are stored in seed banks. The seeds are stored at freezing temperatures in vast underground vaults protected from the outside world. If they are needed in the future, they will be able to grow. Why not create your own seed bank?

REMEMBER, SOME SEEDS ARE POISONOUS! DO NOT EAT ANY SEEDS AND WASH YOUR HANDS AFTER HANDLING THEM.

1. Gather your seeds. Most plants will produce seeds in late summer and autumn. Put them in dry paper envelopes and label each one with the name of the plant, or a description of it, and the date.

2. After two weeks, check that the seeds are dry inside the envelopes. Then put them in their long-term home: a big glass jar is perfect.

3. Place your seed bank in the fridge or freezer. You can take seeds out at any time and try growing them—your seed bank will last for many years to come!

The future of our green planet

New species of plant are still being discovered every year. At the same time, others are being wiped out. There is an urgent challenge to understand how the planet's plants might help us, such as in medicine. We can do this by learning from the people who use plants—they have important local knowledge of them. We can also educate people so that they understand the need to protect plants.

Plants are the key to our survival, but that's not the only reason we should protect them. Nature also has a value all of its own. We share our planet with millions of other species that existed long before we did. We have a duty to protect nature in its many different forms, not just for future generations to enjoy, but for its own sake.

INDEX